MEL BAY'
EASIEST
ROCK
GUITAR
BOOK

By William Bay

1 2 3 4 5 6 7 8 9 0

Mel Bay's Easiest Rock Guitar Book is an ideal way to get started playing contemporary rock and blues guitar. At first, you will learn the basic techniques needed to play rock guitar, such as the slide, the bend, hammer-on, pull-off, and vibrato. Then, you will play a driving bass solo, a rock lead solo, and four rock rhythm chord studies in the keys of E, G, and D. For a more thorough and complete study of rock guitar, or as a follow-up to this book, we recommend *Kids' Rock Guitar Method* book and stereo play-along cassette.

HOW TO HOLD THE GUITAR & PICK

The correct way to hold the guitar.

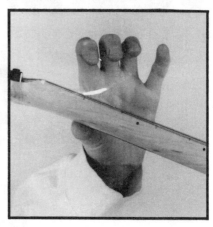

#1

Place your thumb in the middle of the back of the neck.

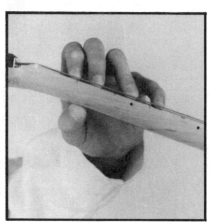

#2

Place your fingers FIRMLY on the string DIRECTLY BEHIND THE FRETS.

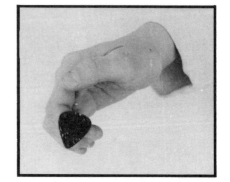

#2

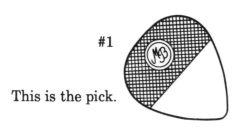

#1

This is the pick.

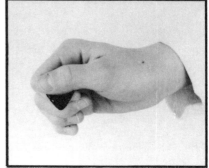

#3

Hold it in this manner, firmly between the thumb and first finger.

Time Signature

4/4 or **C** time = four counts per measure.

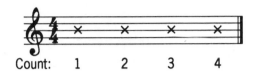

Count: 1   2   3   4

Notes and Rests

Whole Note (Play)	Whole Rest (Rest — Do Not Play)
o	▬
Four Counts	Four Counts
Half Note	**Half Rest**
𝅗𝅥	▬
Two Counts	Two Counts
Quarter Note	**Quarter Rest**
♩	𝄽
One Count	One Count
Eighth Note	**Eighth Rest**
♪ or ♫	𝄾
One Half Count	One Half Count

Count and clap the following exercise.

Count: 1 2 3 4   1 2 3 4   1   2   3   4   1   2   3   4   1 2   3 4

THE SLIDE

The slide is our first effect. The symbol for a slide is this: ╱ To slide into a note, finger a note two frets lower than the note you want to play. Then, after you pick the lower note, quickly slide up to the desired note *without* picking the string again.

For example, to slide into E: Pick this note and then without lifting your finger *and* without picking again slide into E.

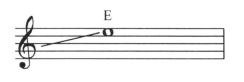

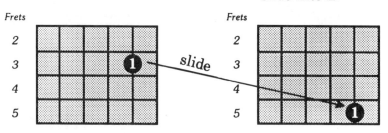

"HAMMER-ON" EFFECT

This is a very important effect for rock lead guitar. To accomplish this effect, you pick one note. Then, without raising your left-hand finger and without picking the string again, you press down hard on a higher note on the same string with a different finger. Usually the first note is fingered with the index finger of your left hand, and the second note is fingered with the left-hand ring finger.

A hammer-on looks like this:

E

Hammer-On

=

① Finger second string, 3rd fret, with the first finger and pick the note.

② Keep first finger down on string and quickly press third finger down on the 5th fret.

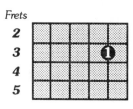

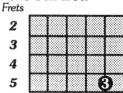

"PULL-OFF"

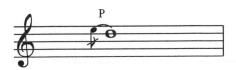

A pull-off looks like this:

A pull-off works in just the opposite way from that of a hammer-on. To play a pull-off, play the higher note first (third finger) and then, while the third finger is still on the higher note, press your first finger down on the desired note (usually 2 frets down). Then pull your first finger off of the string with a snapping motion. This will allow the first-finger note to sound (without picking the string again).

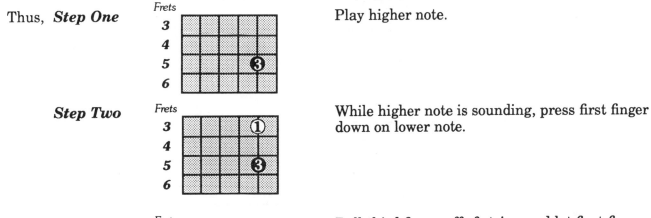

Thus, **Step One**

Play higher note.

Step Two

While higher note is sounding, press first finger down on lower note.

Step Three

Pull third finger off of string and let first-finger note sound.

VIBRATO

Vibrato is a great blues/rock lead guitar effect. It looks like this:

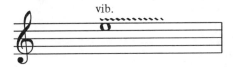

The most widely used method of vibrato is to play a note and then, while you are still holding your left-hand finger down, rock your left hand back and forth (toward the tuning keys and then toward the tailpiece).

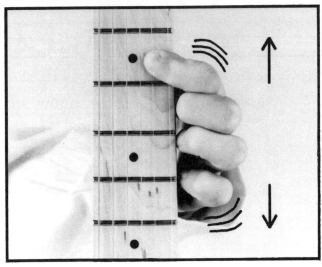

Tablature is a way of writing guitar music which tells you where to find notes. In tablature:

> **Lines = Strings**
>
> **Numbers = Frets**

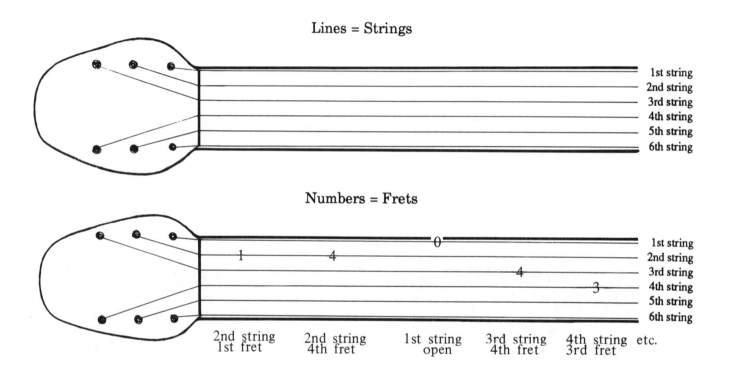

When numbers appear right above one another, more than one note is played at the same time.

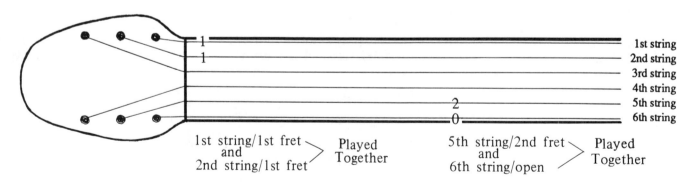

THE BEND

Learning to bend notes is essential to blues/rock lead guitar. To bend a note, finger your note and then push the string towards the sixth string. This raises the pitch. (You will need very light-gauge strings on your guitar to bend notes effectively. Also, you will see that it is easier to bend notes the higher you go up the fingerboard.)

A bend looks like this on your guitar:

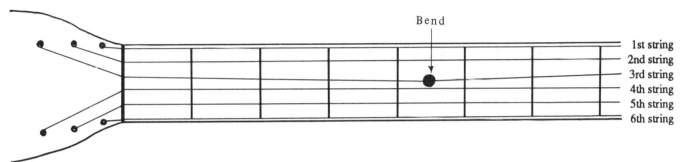

A bend is notated like this:

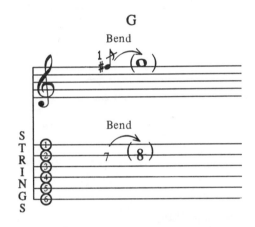

In the above example, you would play second string, 7th fret, and bend the string until the note sounds like the note on second string, 8th fret.

Practice bending these notes:

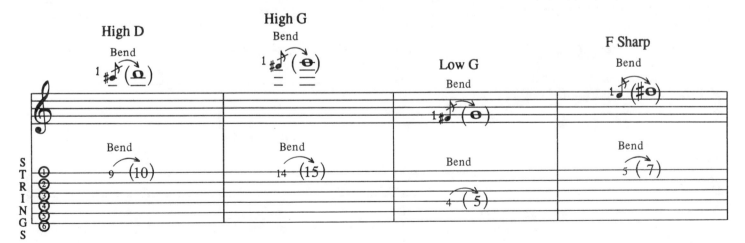

KEY OF E

Driving Bass Solo / Key of E

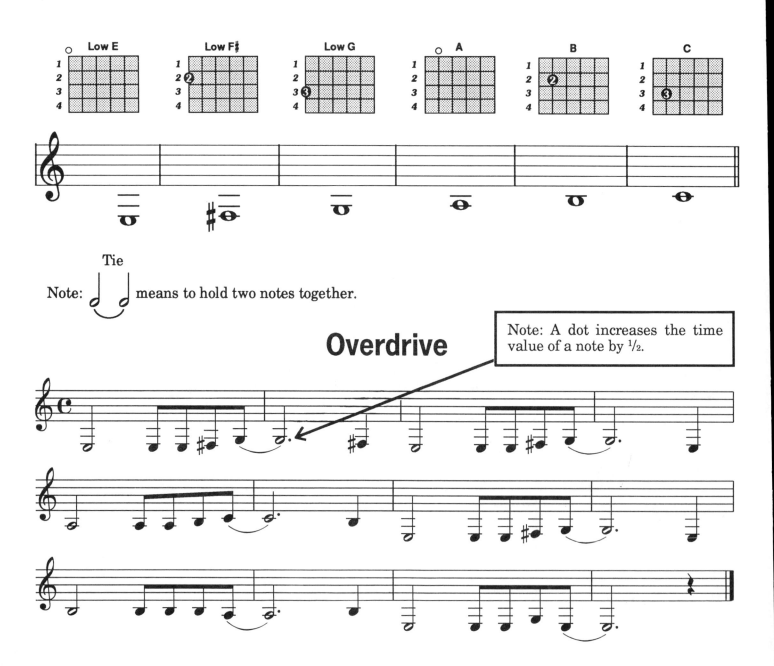

Notes needed:

Tie

Note: ♩⌣♩ means to hold two notes together.

Overdrive

Note: A dot increases the time value of a note by $\frac{1}{2}$.

KEY-OF-E SOLO / LICKS

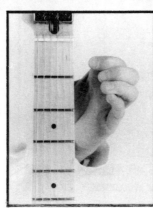

Low E String-Open

Fingerboard position of left hand

Lick #1

Lick #2

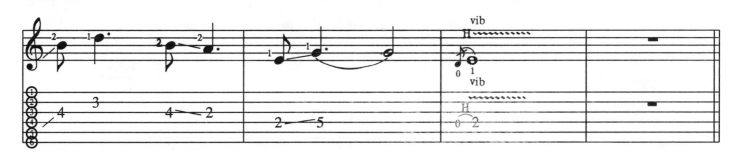

(1) Memorize Licks #1 and #2.

(2) Play Lick #1 twice and then play Lick #2.

Solo #1

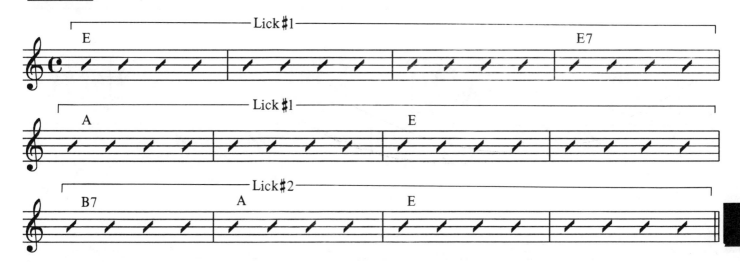

GUIDE TO CHORD DIAGRAMS

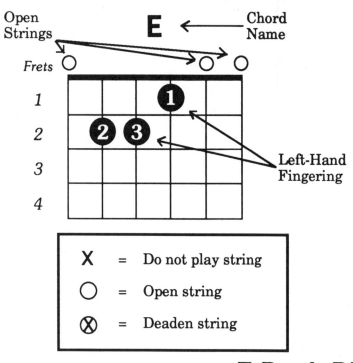

Open Strings

E ← Chord Name

Frets

1

2

3

4

Left-Hand Fingering

X = Do not play string

O = Open string

⊗ = Deaden string

For a complete guide to rock power chords, see page 20.

E Rock Rhythm #1

Basic Rhythm

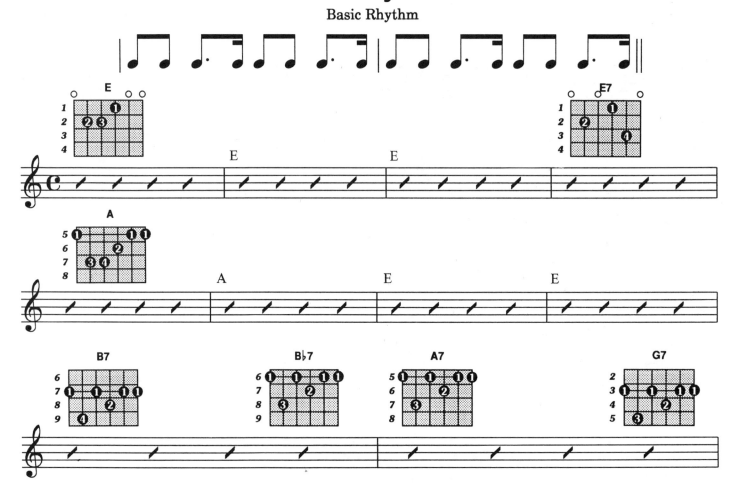

E Rock Rhythm #2

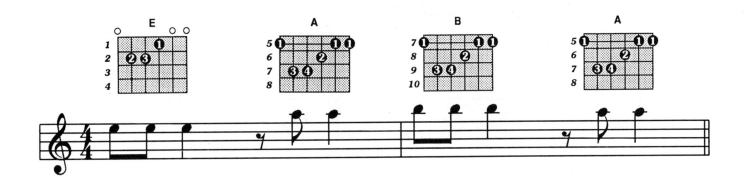

E Rock Rhythm #3

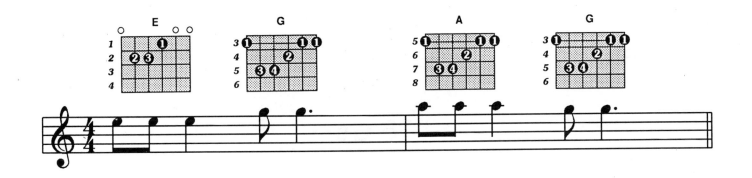

E Rock Rhythm #4

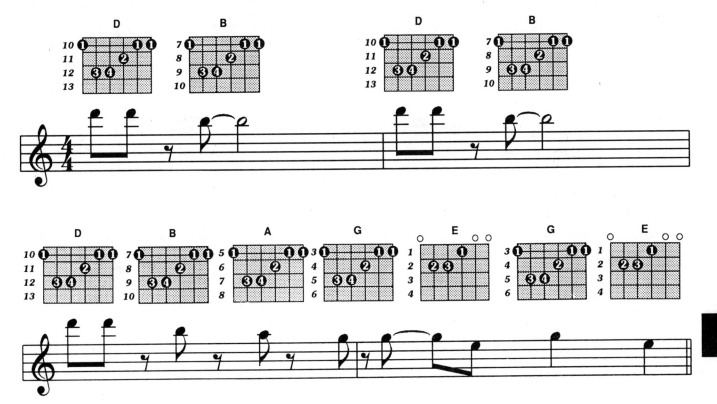

Driving Bass Solo / Key of G

Notes needed:

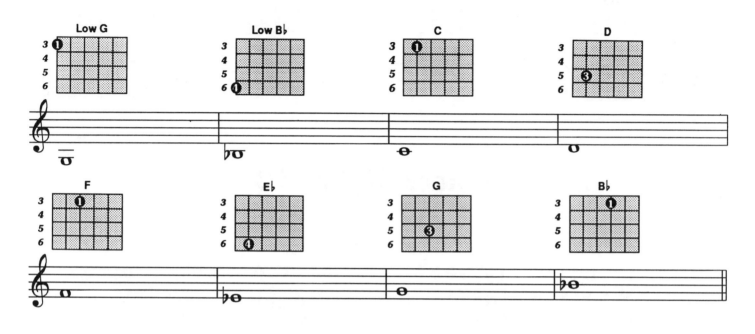

16 G's

KEY-OF-G SOLO / LICKS

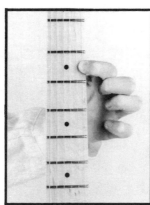

1st string
1st finger
3rd fret

Fingerboard
position of
the left hand

Lick #1

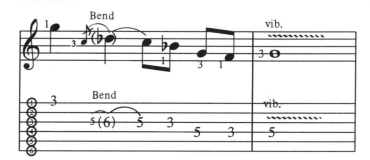

Lick #2

Lick #3

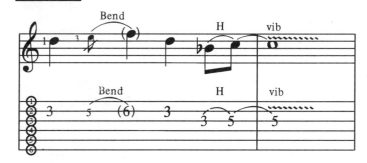

① Memorize Licks #1, #2, and #3.

② Play Lick #1 twice and Lick #2 once.
Play Lick #1again. Then play Lick #3.
End with Lick #1.

Solo #1

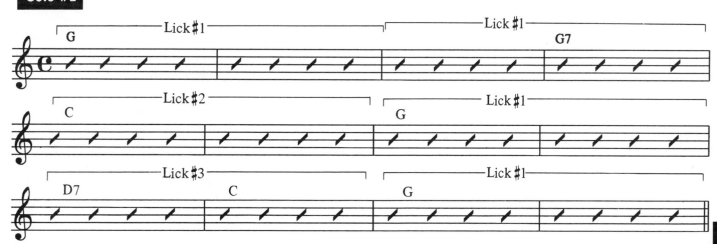

13

Basic Rhythm

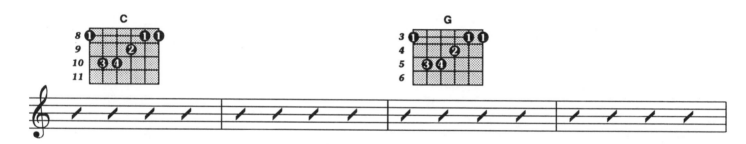

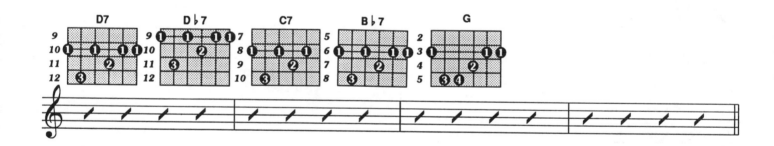

G Rock Rhythm #2

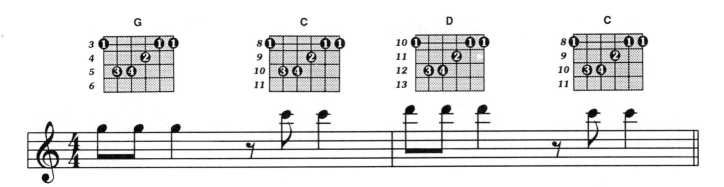

G Rock Rhythm #3

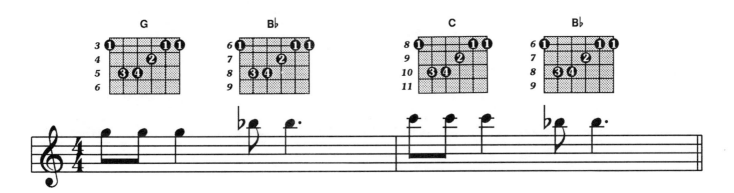

G Rock Rhythm #4

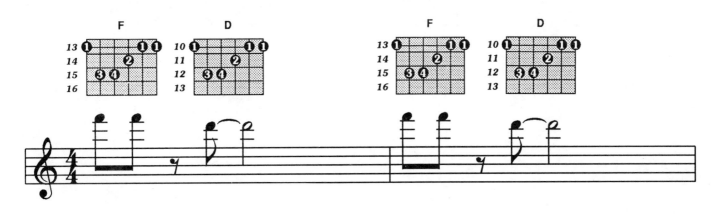

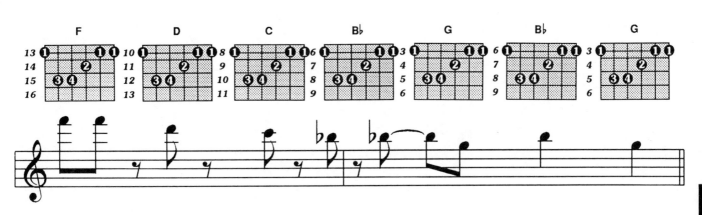

KEY OF D

Driving Bass Solo / Key of D

Notes needed:

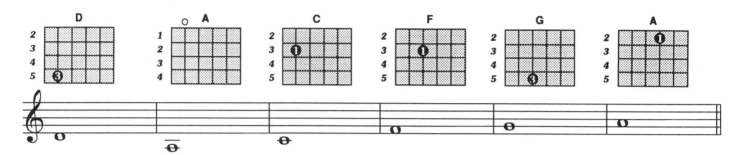

Drivin' D

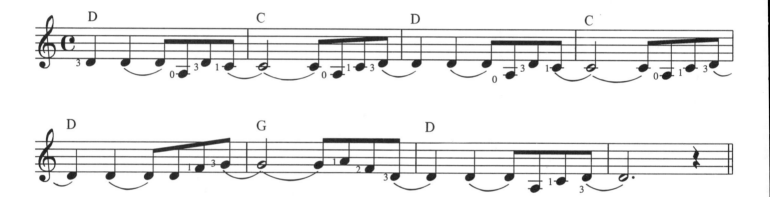

Lick #1

Lick #2

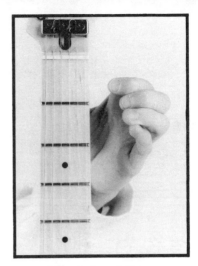

4th string / Open

① Memorize Licks #1, #2, and #3.
② Play Lick #1 twice, then Lick #2, Lick #1, Lick #3, and end with Lick #1.

Lick #3

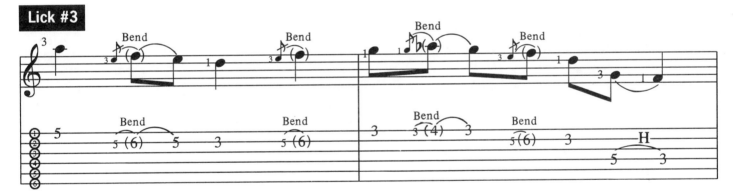

Solo #1

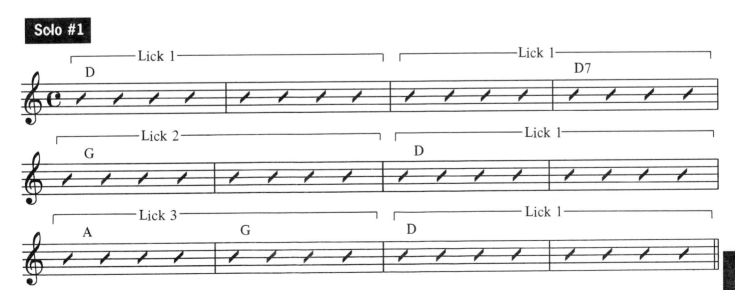

Basic Rhythm

Now try the above using the following power chords:

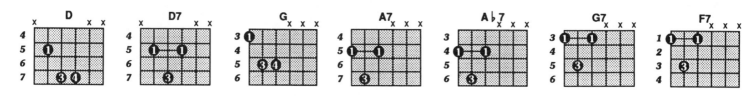

D Rock Rhythm #2

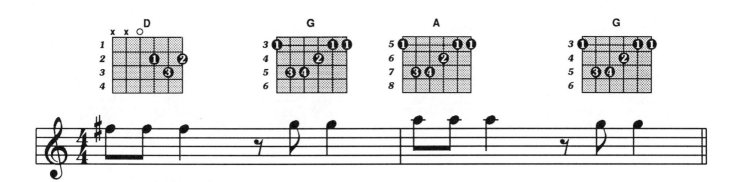

D Rock Rhythm #3

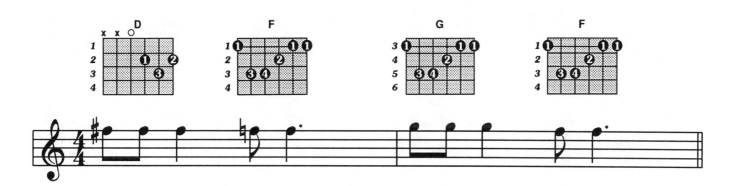

D Rock Rhythm #4

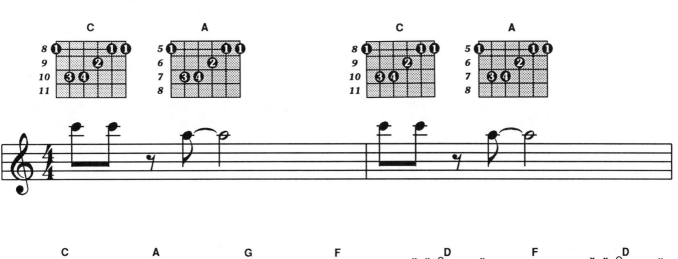

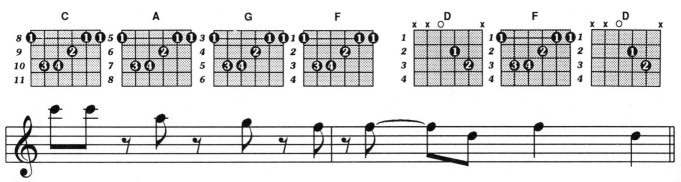

ROCK POWER CHORDS

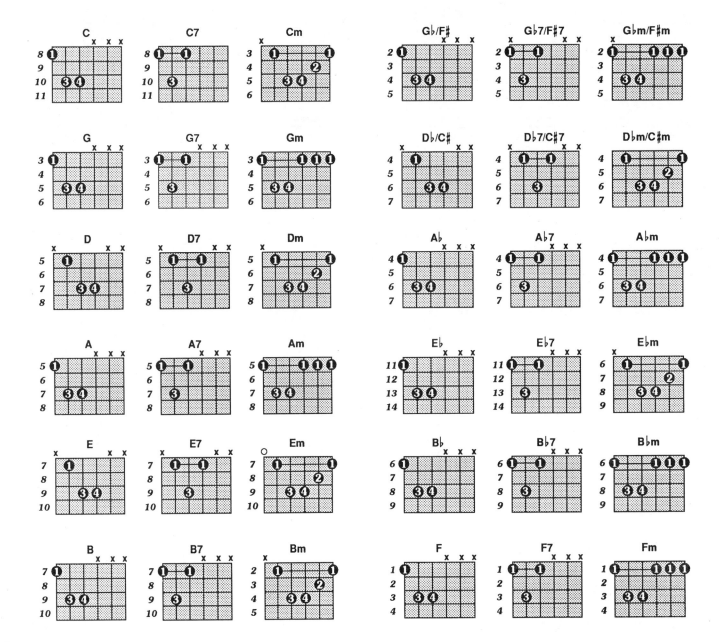